# *Still the Greatest:*
## *Muhammad Ali*

**Adam Grant**

Some of the dialog in this play has been invented. But
the story is based on true events.

**SCHOLASTIC INC.**
New York   Toronto   London   Auckland   Sydney
Mexico City   New Delhi   Hong Kong

**Cover photograph by
©Thomas Hoepker/ Magnum Photos**

**Interior illustrations by
Chuck Frazier**

1  2  3  4  5  6  7  8  9  10        23        10  09  08  07  06  05  04  03  02  01

# *Characters*

**Narrator 1**

**Joe Martin,** a police officer and boxing instructor

**Narrator 2**

**Cassius Clay,** a young boxer

**Tony,** Martin's assistant

**Rudy,** Clay's brother

**Stranger**

**Lunch Counterman**

**Angelo Dundee,** Ali's trainer

**Sonny Liston,** heavyweight champion 1962-1964

**Sportswriter 1**

**Howard Cosell,** a sports announcer

**Muhammad Ali,** Cassius Clay's new name

**Sportswriter 2**

**Reporter**

**Lawyer 1**

*(continued on next page)*

**Lawyer 2**

**Zairian Woman**

**Zairian Man**

**George Foreman,** heavyweight champion
1973-1974 and 1994-1995

**Ring Announcer 1**

**Ring Announcer 2**

# Scene 1

**Narrator 1:** In 1954, in Louisville, Kentucky, a police officer named Joe Martin strolls through his basement boxing gym. Boys of all ages are lifting weights, hitting punching bags, and skipping rope.

**Martin:** Come on, Jed, use your jab!

**Narrator 2:** The door swings open, and a skinny 12-year-old African American kid races in.

**Clay:** Are you Joe Martin, the policeman?

**Martin:** That's right. Who are you?

**Clay:** I'm Cassius Clay. My bike was stolen. It's red. You've got to get it back for me.

**Martin:** Calm down, son. I'll fill out a police

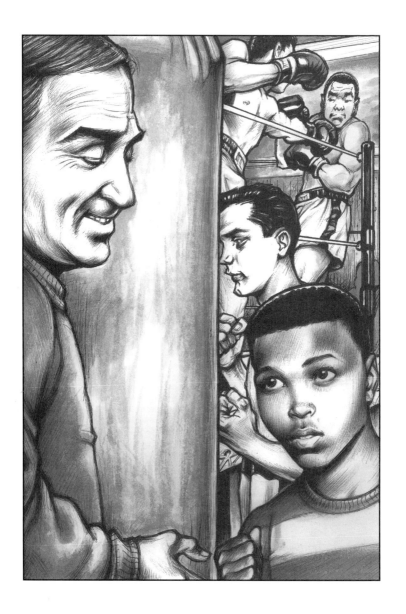

report, and I doubt we'll get your bike back.

**Clay:** Then I guess I'll just have to find the guy who stole it and whup him myself.

**Martin:** You know how to box?

**Clay:** Nothing to it, man. I could whup all these chumps in here.

**Martin:** It's not as easy as all that, son. You gotta be quick and tough. Come back sometime and try it out.

**Clay:** Yeah. Maybe I'll do that. I have to check my busy schedule.

How would you describe young Cassius Clay?

# Scene 2

**Narrator 1:** A few weeks later, Cassius starts going to Martin's gym. He makes an impression on Joe and his staff right away. One day, Joe Martin is watching Clay when his assistant walks up.

**Martin:** Hey, Tony, what do you think of the Clay kid?

**Tony:** He's not much of a boxer. But he's a character. A real smart aleck.

**Martin:** But there's something special about him. And he works harder than any kid in here.

**Narrator 2:** Clay improves fast. Soon he is fighting on a local Louisville TV show called

Tomorrow's Champions and winning. But as his boxing skills get better, his ego gets bigger.

**Martin:** Hey kid. Nice job Thursday night against O'Keefe.

**Clay:** I know. I'm the best fighter in Louisville. I'm going to be Golden Gloves champ. Then I'll win the Olympics, turn pro, and be the heavyweight champ.

**Martin:** Calm down, kid.

**Narrator 1:** Martin smiles and mumbles to himself.

**Martin:** Man, what a mouth.

How do you think Joe Martin feels about Cassius Clay?

# Scene 3

**Narrator 2:** Clay takes boxing very seriously. Every moment becomes part of his training. His whole life becomes about boxing. He thinks about it all the time.

**Narrator 1:** Even when he hangs out with his brother, Rudy, he is thinking about boxing.

**Clay:** Hey, Rudy, throw some rocks at me.

**Rudy:** No, man. Not again.

**Clay:** Come on. It's good for me. I'm too quick and pretty to get hit. If you can't hit me with a rock, then nobody can hit me with a fist.

**Rudy:** You ain't so great.

**Clay:** Oh no? I'm gonna be the heavyweight champ.

**Rudy:** Champ or chump, you'd better learn to keep your mouth shut if you want to stay alive.

**Clay:** What are you talking about?

**Rudy:** Cassius, White people aren't going to let you show them up all the time and run your mouth. Wake up.

**Clay:** No, you wake up. You got no pride. I'm Black. I'm handsome. I'm quick and strong, and I'm going to be great. And nobody can tell me who to be. I'm free to be whoever I want to be.

**Rudy:** All right. Come on. I changed my mind. I'd love to throw some rocks at you.

**Narrator 2:** Rudy starts throwing rocks at Cassius. But Cassius is too fast. He dodges every one.

How are Cassius and his brother different?

# Scene 4

**Narrator 1:** By age 18, Cassius Clay has won just about every amateur boxing title he could possibly win.

**Narrator 2:** Then, in 1960, the boy from Louisville wins a gold medal at the Olympics in Rome! He returns home to a hero's welcome. He is the guest of honor at dinners, and he even meets the mayor.

**Narrator 1:** But not everyone treats him well.

**Stranger:** Get over here, boy. Let me see that gold medal.

**Narrator 2:** People call him "boy." They do not treat him with respect. In 1960, there are still segregation laws in the South.

**Narrator 1:** Blacks and Whites are separated in most places. Sometimes it's hard for the Olympian to find a place to eat lunch.

**Lunch Counterman:** I don't care who he is. I'm not serving him. Look at the sign. It says this here place is for Whites only.

**Clay:** Man, I don't believe this. I've got the Olympic gold medal around my neck!

**Rudy:** I told you before, some of these folks aren't going to like you no matter what you do. You better get used to it.

**Narrator 2:** Cassius is so proud of his medal that he sleeps with it on. But one day, he shocks everyone by throwing his medal into the Ohio River.

**Rudy:** Are you nuts? What did you do that for?

**Clay:** I loved that medal more than anything I've ever had. I thought it made me somebody. But look how people are treating me. Like I'm nothing.

**Rudy:** But you earned that medal. You deserve it.

**Clay:** People call me "boy" when they ask for my autograph. They wouldn't talk to me at all if I didn't have that medal. Well, now I don't have it. But I'm going to make those people respect me. I'm going to be heavyweight champion of the world. And then they're all going to deal with me on my terms.

Why does Cassius throw his medal in the river?

# Scene 5

**Narrator 1:** Clay begins his pro boxing career after the Olympics in 1960. In the next four years, Clay wins 18 fights in a row. Then he starts working with a famous boxing trainer named Angelo Dundee.

**Narrator 2:** People are talking about Cassius Clay. They talk about his boxing. But they are more interested in Clay as a person than as a fighter.

**Narrator 1:** Before each fight, he dazzles the press with his wit, charm and nerve. He even speaks to reporters in poetry.

**Clay:** This is the story about a man
With iron fists and a beautiful tan.
He talks a lot and boasts indeed
Of a power punch and blinding speed.

**Narrator 2:** Clay is funny and bold when he speaks about his fights. Sometimes he even predicts what will happen.

**Narrator 1:** In 1962, Clay fights a former champion named Archie Moore.

**Clay:**  Archie's been living off the fat of
    the land
I'm here to give him his pension plan.
When you come to the fight, don't
    block the door
'Cause you'll all go home after
    round four.

**Narrator 2:** Sure enough, Clay knocks out Moore in the fourth round. Not every prediction comes true, but Clay keeps winning. Still, nobody thinks he's ready to fight the heavyweight champion, Sonny Liston. That is nobody except Clay.

**Narrator 1:** Even Clay's trainer, Angelo Dundee, doesn't want him to fight Liston. Liston is the scariest boxer to come along in a long time. He learned to fight in prison and he always beats up his opponents badly.

**Dundee:** You're not ready, kid. Wait a while. You'll be the greatest someday.

**Clay:** I could whup that big ugly bear right now.

**Narrator 2:** Finally, Clay takes matters into his own hands.

**Clay:** Come on, Rudy, we're driving to Denver to visit Sonny Liston.

**Rudy:** Are you crazy? We're in Chicago. That's two days' drive.

**Narrator 1:** But Cassius convinces Rudy to take the drive. Along the way, they call several reporters.

**Narrator 2:** They arrive at Liston's house at two in the morning and knock at the door. Liston comes out in his bathrobe. He is very angry.

**Liston:** What do you want?

**Narrator 1:** Clay starts dancing around Liston's front lawn. He yells at a group of reporters who have gathered.

**Clay:** I am the greatest! Sonny Liston is scared

to fight me! I'll whup that big ugly bear!

**Narrator 2:** Liston shakes his head and mutters to himself.

**Liston:** All right, I'll fight him. I'm going to *kill* that kid.

**Narrator 1:** A few days later, Sonny Liston signs to fight Cassius Clay for the heavyweight championship of the world. Only one person on the planet thinks Clay can win. Again, that would be Clay. And he gladly tells every reporter he can find.

**Clay:** Sonny Liston is nothing. The man can't talk. The man can't fight. He needs boxing lessons. And since he's gonna be fighting me, he needs falling lessons.

**Narrator 2:** The press doesn't give Clay much of a chance. He's the underdog.

**Sportswriter 1:** Cassius is crazy to even think about entering the ring against a deadly fighting machine like Sonny Liston.

**Narrator 1:** But nothing can shake Clay's confidence. The fight is on. And on February

25, 1964, Clay comes out swinging. Howard Cosell is the announcer that night.

**Cosell:** Ladies and gentlemen, I don't believe it. Clay is handling Liston. He's just too fast for the older champ.

**Narrator 2:** But just before the fifth round, Clay screams to his corner.

**Clay:** Something's in my eyes. They're burning! I can't see! Stop the fight!

**Narrator 1:** Clay's trainer, Angelo Dundee, can't figure out what is wrong. He sprays water in Clay's eyes and wipes them out.

**Dundee:** You gotta go back out there. This is for the title. Just stay away from him. Run!

**Narrator 2:** In a display of amazing courage, Clay stumbles blindly into the ring.

**Narrator 1:** For most of the round, he dances away from the champ, dodging punches and bravely taking the rest. Finally, his eyes clear. He can see again. He comes back and wins the sixth round.

**Cosell:** This is hard to figure. Clay looked like he'd about had it. . .

**Narrator 2:** Suddenly, there is a roar from the crowd.

**Cosell:** Wait a minute! Sonny Liston is not coming out for the seventh round! He's out! The new world heavyweight champion is Cassius Clay!

**Narrator 1:** There is chaos inside the ring. The crowd is electric. Sonny Liston is sitting in his corner, shaking his head.

**Liston:** He was just too fast.

**Narrator 2:** Cassius Clay stands at the ropes, shouting to reporters.

**Clay:** I am the greatest! I am the prettiest thing that ever lived! I can't be beat! I shook up the world! I want justice!

What happened to Cassius Clay in the fifth round?

# Scene 6

**Narrator 1:** Almost nobody had expected Cassius Clay to beat Sonny Liston. But everyone is shocked at what he does next.

**Clay:** I have an announcement. I have joined the Nation of Islam. I have changed my name to Muhammad Ali. The name means "worthy of all praise most high." I've left behind "Cassius Clay the Clown" to become "Muhammad the Wise Man."

**Narrator 2:** The Nation of Islam or Black Muslims, as many call them, is made up of African Americans who have converted to a religion called Islam.

**Narrator 1:** In the 1960s, most Americans are suspicious of the African Americans who are in the Nation of Islam.

**Narrator 2:** Many believe the group to be against Whites. But Ali defends them.

**Ali:** The religion is called Islam. The name means peace. That's what it's about.

**Narrator 1:** Soon, a war of words has begun between the young champion and the press. They even refuse to use his new name.

**Sportswriter 2:** Cassius Clay, or whatever he wants to be called, is thumbing his nose at America.

**Ali:** I don't hate America. This is my home. But it's not right that I'm the world heavyweight champion, and there are neighborhoods in my own country that I can't even live in.

**Sportswriter 1:** Mr. Clay should decide if he wants to be a boxer or a spokesman for a religion. If Mr. Clay can't act appropriately, he should have to give back his title.

**Ali:** As heavyweight champion, I don't have to do anything except be a nice, clean gentleman. I don't have to be who you want me to be. I'm free to be who I want.

**Narrator 2:** Never before has an athlete stood up to the press the way Ali does. The press criticizes him. But Ali ignores them.

**Narrator 1:** Ali goes on a goodwill tour of Africa, where he is greeted as a hero. He returns and wins many more fights.

**Narrator 2:** Soon, the press begins to admit that he is a great boxer. And although many people don't like what Ali says, some start to admire him for standing up for his beliefs.

Do you agree with what Ali said to the press? Why or why not?

# Scene 7

**Narrator 1:** In February 1966, Ali receives a draft notice from the U.S. Army. Reporters go to his house in Miami to see what the Champ has to say.

**Reporter:** How do you feel about the war in Vietnam?

**Ali:** I am against war because of my religious beliefs.

**Reporter:** What do you think about our enemy, the Vietcong?

**Ali:** Man, I got no quarrel with them Vietcong!

**Narrator 2:** In 1966, many Americans feel it's important to support the war in Vietnam. Every newspaper prints what Ali said. People

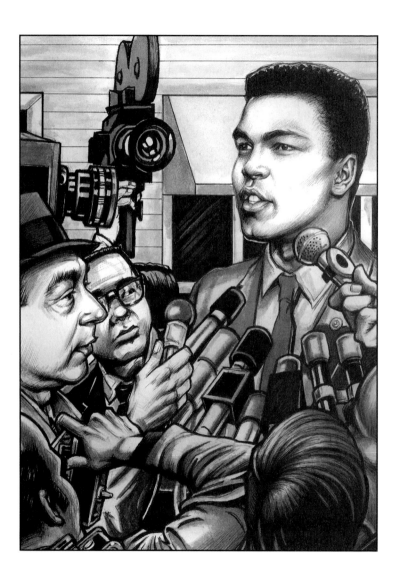

accuse him of siding with the enemy.

**Narrator 1:** Overnight, Ali becomes one of the most hated people in America. A year later, Ali formally refuses to go into the Army.

**Ali:** The laws of my religion do not allow me to support this war. If I have to lose my titles and millions of dollars, so be it. If I have to go to jail, I'll go to jail.

**Narrator 2:** Within an hour, Ali is stripped of his titles and banned from boxing.

**Narrator 1:** He also faces a criminal charge of draft evasion. He could go to prison. His lawyers give him practical advice.

**Lawyer 1:** Listen, Champ, all you have to do is enlist. They won't make you fight.

**Lawyer 2:** Can't you just put on a uniform and put on boxing shows? You know, entertain the troops?

**Ali:** As a Muslim minister, it is against my beliefs to support this war. How can I tell the children of the world to stand up for their beliefs if I don't stand up for my own? I will not do it.

**Narrator 2:** Ali is convicted of draft evasion and sentenced to five years in jail. But his lawyers keep him out on bail while they appeal his case.

**Narrator 1:** For three and a half years, the court case continues. Banned from boxing, Ali studies his religion and makes a modest living giving speeches.

**Narrator 2:** Meanwhile, boxing searches for a new heavyweight champion. Ali just watches.

**Ali:** Let the man that wins go to the backwoods of Georgia or to Sweden or Africa. Let him go to an elementary school, or a street corner where boys are playing and see what they say. Everybody knows that I am champion. My ghost will haunt the streets and arenas, whispering "Ali. . . Ali . . ."

What happens when Ali refuses to join the army?

# Scene 8

**Narrator 1:** Finally, in 1970, Ali is allowed to fight again when New York State grants him a boxing license. Within a year, the Supreme Court dismisses the criminal case against him. Ali is free. He is back in the ring. But his career has suffered.

**Narrator 2:** Ali loses in his first bid to win back the heavyweight title, and he has to fight 14 times before he gets another shot at it. His chance comes against a new heavyweight champion, George Foreman. The fight takes place in Zaire, Africa.

**Ali:** It's gonna be a "Rumble in the Jungle!"

**Narrator 1:** Ali travels to Zaire to fight Foreman. He is greeted in Zaire by thousands of adoring fans. They scream and wave, and talk to the TV news cameras, which follow Ali everywhere.

**Zairian Woman:** We love Ali for who he is, not just as a boxer.

**Zairian Man:** To see a Black man in America stand up for himself gave us all courage and made us proud. He is our champion.

**Narrator 2:** In Zaire, Ali is more than just a fighter. He is an ambassador of goodwill. He gives many in the West their first glimpse of Africa.

**Ali:** Africa. The homeland of my people. It's amazing. Everything here is run by Black people. Everyone should see this.

**Narrator 1:** But Ali is there to fight George Foreman, who is big, strong, and young. His record is 40 wins, 37 by knockout. He has no losses.

**Narrator 2:** Once again, nobody gives Ali a chance. And once again, Ali has something to say to those who doubt him.

**Ali:** George Foreman don't stand a chance.

When I get finished going upside his head, he'll have so many nicks and cuts it will look like he had a bad morning shave.

**Narrator 1:** But Foreman has plenty of confidence, too.

**Foreman:** The guys I fight don't worry about losing. They worry about getting hurt.

**Narrator 2:** Between training sessions, Ali visits hundreds of people a day. All over Zaire, he wanders into towns and villages. People crowd and push just to touch him or shake his hand.

**Ali:** These are my people. And I am one of them. It's good for them to see that a big, strong, rich, handsome Black hero like me cares about them.

**Narrator 1:** On October 30, 1974, millions of people around the world watch as Ali meets Foreman in the ring.

**Narrator 2:** Most people expect Foreman to win by an early knockout. And it looks like they are right.

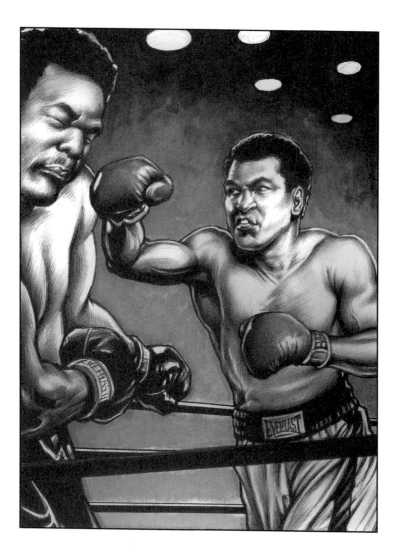

**Ring Announcer 1:** Ali is on the ropes again! He's taking punch after punch to the body! How much more can he take?

**Ring Announcer 2:** I expected Ali to use his speed to keep away from the champ. But he's been trapped on the ropes all night.

**Narrator 1:** After round six, Ali's corner men are worried.

**Dundee:** He's killing you! Why don't you keep away from him?

**Ali:** He's getting tired. He's punching himself out. I've got him.

**Dundee:** Nobody can take that many punches. You'll get killed.

**Ali:** I know what I'm doing. He's tiring himself out.

**Narrator 2:** By the seventh round, Foreman's punches are no longer strong enough to hurt Ali. Ali starts talking.

**Ali:** Is that all you got, George? I heard you could punch.

**Narrator 1:** Foreman is tired and frustrated. He swings wildly at Ali, leaving himself unprotected.

**Ring Announcer 1:** Look at Ali go! One, two, three — he just got Foreman with three left jabs. Now a right! Foreman has dropped.

**Ring Announcer 2:** I don't believe it! Foreman is not getting up. That's it. Ali is the world heavyweight champion again!

**Narrator 2:** The stadium is in chaos. People are jumping, yelling and chanting Ali's name. Ali is shouting to the press.

**Ali:** I told you I would do it! But did you listen? I am the greatest of ALL TIME!

What strategy did Ali use to beat Foreman?

# Scene 9

**Narrator 1:** Ali defends his title in 10 successful fights during the 1970s. Then he loses it to another Olympian, Leon Spinks. Seven months later, Ali wins the heavyweight title back again. He becomes the first boxer to win it three times.

**Narrator 2:** But by the late 1970s, Ali's speech is beginning to slur. His friends beg him to retire. They worry that he's suffering brain damage from taking punches to the head.

**Narrator 1:** Ali returns to the ring for two more fights. He loses both of them. In 1981, Muhammad Ali finally retires from boxing. Doctors discover that Ali had Parkinson's disease. It is a nervous disorder that can be caused by repeated blows to the head.

**Narrator 2:** Since his retirement, Ali has made himself an ambassador for world peace. He travels all over the globe, meeting people and giving his name, his money and his time to fight poverty and injustice.

**Ali:** People say I had a full life, but I ain't dead yet. All of my boxing, all of my running around, all of my publicity was just the start of my life. Now my life is really starting. I'm still fighting. Only now I'm fighting Parkinson's. But that's not all. I'm also fighting injustice, fighting racism, fighting crime, fighting illiteracy, fighting poverty, and using this face the world knows so well, to fight for the truth.

Of all the things Ali has done, what do you think took the most courage?

# Epilogue

Muhammad Ali finally has the respect he fought for and richly deserves.

In 1996, he had the honor of lighting the Olympic torch during the opening ceremonies of the games in Atlanta, Georgia. And in 2001, President Bill Clinton awarded him the Presidential Citizen's Medal. He received this award for his athletic achievements and for his struggle against racism.

The Muhammad Ali Center in Ali's hometown of Louisville, Kentucky, was started to preserve and share the champion's ideals. The center's mission is "to promote respect, hope, and understanding, and to inspire adults and children everywhere to be as great as they can be."

# *Rigoberta Menchú:*
## *La voz de su pueblo*
## *(The Voice of Her People)*

**John Rearick and Debra Hess**

This play is based on the book
*I, Rigoberta: An Indian Woman in Guatemala*
by Rigoberta Menchú.

**SCHOLASTIC INC.**
New York   Toronto   London   Auckland   Sydney
Mexico City   New Delhi   Hong Kong

# *Characters*

**Narrator 1**

**Narrator 2**

**Mother,** of Rigoberta

**Father,** of Rigoberta

**Rigoberta Menchú,** a young Quiché girl

**Overseer,** at the coffee plantation

**Plantation Owner**

**Plantation Owner's Wife**

**Government Official**

**Petrocinio,** one of Rigoberta's brothers

**Soldier**

**Army Captain**

**Writer**

## Scene 1

**Narrator 1:** In 1959, in the mountains of Central America, in a country called Guatemala, a child was born. Her name was Rigoberta Menchú. Rigoberta was a Quiché (Key-CHAY) Indian. Like most of her people, her family lived off the land. But, they did not always have enough money for food and other necessities.

**Narrator 2:** And like most Quichés, Rigoberta had only a little schooling. Many others had none. This meant that most Indians could not speak Spanish, the country's official language. Not knowing Spanish kept them from getting an education or a good job.

**Narrator 1:** In spite of being poor, Rigoberta's

parents taught her to love her Quiché heritage.

**Narrator 2:** They brought her up to love the mountains where she lived. They taught her to be proud of the traditions of her people.

**Mother:** Rigoberta, my child, we are poor compared to many people who live in the city. But we are surrounded by the most beautiful mountains. Don't ever forget that you are a Quiché Indian. No one can ever take that from you.

**Father:** Your mother is right, Rigoberta. You must always wear the clothes of our people, and eat the food our people have always eaten. You must speak our language and keep our traditions alive.

**Rigoberta:** But why? Other people don't have so many special ceremonies.

**Father:** Our traditions keep us connected to our ancestors. That's more important than life itself.

**Mother:** And you must always keep our traditions secret, Rigoberta.

**Rigoberta:** But why?

**Mother:** They belong to our people. They have been passed down to us for over a thousand years. They make us who we are. And that is something to be very proud of, Rigoberta.

What did Rigoberta's parents teach her?

## Scene 2

**Narrator 1:** Rigoberta loved where she lived. There were mountains and trees everywhere.

**Narrator 2:** But it was hard for Rigoberta's parents to earn money living in the mountains. One day, when Rigoberta was eight years old, her parents called her to them.

**Mother:** Rigoberta, get ready. Tomorrow we have to go down the mountain.

**Rigoberta:** Why do we have to go?

**Father:** Now that we've planted our own corn, we have to go to the coffee plantation. It is harvest time. We will pick someone else's crops to earn a little money.

**Mother:** Maybe, if we are lucky, we can harvest

the food we have planted when we get back.

**Narrator 1:** Rigoberta's whole family climbed down the mountain and went to the coffee plantation.

**Narrator 2:** While her father and older brothers and sisters went to pick coffee, Rigoberta stayed behind to help her mother cook and take care of the baby. But she was not happy.

**Rigoberta:** Father, I am tired of watching my baby brother all the time. I can pick coffee just as well as anyone. Let me work, too!

**Father:** Do you know what you are asking? Our work is very hard. We pick coffee all day and earn almost nothing. Someday, I am going to try to change this.

**Rigoberta:** Why don't you make any money if you work all day?

**Father:** The pay is low, and the work is difficult and slow. The overseers watch us like hawks to make sure we don't hurt a leaf on the coffee plants. To them, the plants are

more valuable than people.

**Rigoberta:** Let me help you, Father.

**Mother:** Rigoberta, you are only eight years old. Stay with me and help me cook. Who will watch the baby if you pick coffee?

**Rigoberta:** I want to pick coffee! I am old enough to help make money for our family!

**Mother:** But Rigoberta . . .

**Rigoberta:** Please. I know I can do it.

**Father:** All right. I give up. You can pick coffee with us.

**Narrator 1:** From that day on, Rigoberta went each morning to pick coffee. The work was so tiring that sometimes she fell asleep under a coffee bush.

**Narrator 2:** She learned to work fast, but she also learned about the suffering of others.

**Rigoberta:** Mother, look at those babies over there. Why are their stomachs so swollen? What have they been eating?

**Mother:** Their stomachs are swollen because

they haven't had anything to eat.

**Rigoberta:** But this is a big plantation. There is plenty of space to grow food.

**Mother:** Here, the owners grow coffee and cotton instead of corn. They make money by selling these products to other countries. They don't use this land to grow food.

**Rigoberta:** That doesn't make sense to me, Mother. Babies are starving. They should grow food. And there is another thing that I don't understand.

**Mother:** What is it, child?

**Rigoberta:** Why do Father and the other men look so angry sometimes?

**Mother:** When children don't have enough to eat, their parents become filled with sadness. They forget how our ancestors behaved. You must always remember your ancestors, Rigoberta. Remember what they say in our tribe: "Anyone who forgets their ancestors' ways or stops dressing as they dressed is on the road to ruin."

**Rigoberta:** I'll remember, Mother.

How does Rigoberta feel about the starving children?

# Scene 3

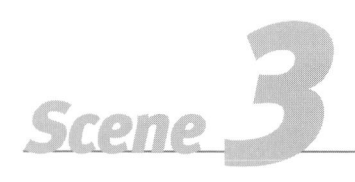

**Narrator 1:** One day, while working on the plantation, Rigoberta asked her mother about her brother, who died before she was born.

**Rigoberta:** Mother, what happened to my brother? Tell me the story again.

**Mother:** Your brother was crying all the time, and his stomach was getting bigger and bigger, but I could do nothing. If I had stopped working to care for him, I would have lost my job. Then we wouldn't have had earned enough money to eat.

**Rigoberta:** Wouldn't anyone help you?

**Mother:** Our Indian neighbors had barely enough food to feed their own families. We

borrowed money from the plantation to pay for medicine, but your brother died anyway. We asked if we could bury his body on the plantation.

**Overseer:** You can bury that body here, but you'll have to pay a special tax. You already owe us for the medicine you wasted on that kid. And if you miss any more work, you'll be fired.

**Mother:** The years passed. But we couldn't save enough money to pay the money we owed. The plantation owners got angry.

**Overseer:** You're fired! Take your kids and get out of here right now. And, by the way, you still owe us for the medicine.

**Mother:** So, we returned to the mountains. We returned without money, without food, and without your brother.

**Narrator 2:** Rigoberta's mother had tears in her eyes.

**Rigoberta:** This isn't fair, Mother. I have to do something.

**Mother:** What can you do, Rigoberta? You are only ten years old.

**Rigoberta:** Maybe if I could learn some more Spanish, at least I could talk to people outside our village. Maybe if we all get together, we could find a way to make things better.

**Mother:** That is a nice thought. But school costs money. Maybe someday we will be able to find a way.

How does Rigoberta hope to help her people?

# Scene

**Narrator 1:** One day, a plantation owner asked Rigoberta's father if Rigoberta could work as a maid in his big house.

**Owner:** Your daughter will have it easy. She will learn to read, write, and speak Spanish. Then she won't be stuck with only your Indian talk.

**Narrator 2:** When Rigoberta learned of the job offer, she begged her father to let her take it.

**Father:** No. Those rich people will only treat you badly. You will learn Spanish and the ways of those city folks. You will forget about us and our ways.

**Rigoberta:** Please, Father. I don't want to work in the fields anymore. I want to learn

Spanish. I promise not to forget our ways. I want to find a way to help our people.

**Narrator 1:** So Rigoberta went to work in the plantation owner's house.

**Plantation Owner's Wife:** I can't believe how dirty you are, Rigoberta! Look at your feet. Haven't you ever worn shoes? You are going to embarrass me in front of my friends. I guess I'll have to give you some new clothes, but it will come out of your pay!

**Narrator 2:** Rigoberta earned very little money working for the plantation owner's wife. She started to learn Spanish, but once she could understand what was being said, she almost wished that she hadn't.

**Plantation Owner's Wife:** These Indians are always so dirty and lazy. You just can't get a day's work out of them. And they steal!

**Narrator 2:** Finally, Rigoberta couldn't take it anymore.

**Rigoberta:** I have to go back to my family.

**Plantation Owner's Wife:** Why? We love you!

Please stay! We'll increase your pay.

**Rigoberta:** Thank you. But you've done enough for me already.

Why did Rigoberta decide to return home?

# Scene

**Narrator 1:** While Rigoberta was working in the city, the government and the big landowners came to take land away from the Indian people. Rigoberta's father took part in a protest.

**Narrator 2:** Rigoberta's father got involved with the struggle for Indian rights. This made the government angry. One day, a government offical came to the mountains. He announced that the government was taking over some property in the village.

**Father:** We made these little farms out of nothing. We barely raise enough corn to feed our families on this land. But it is our land. It is land that we've sweated over.

**Government Official:** We decide who owns this land.

**Father:** Yes, but it is only after our people clear a patch of land and make the earth grow food that the big landowners show up and take it away.

**Government Official:** You Indians just don't understand.

**Father:** No, you don't understand how important this land is to us.

**Government Official:** If I were you, I wouldn't make such a fuss. You'll wind up in jail—or worse!

**Narrator 1:** That night, Rigoberta's father gathered his family around him.

**Father:** This cause is important. And I know that if anything happens to me, you will all carry on the fight for our rights!

What did Rigoberta's father want the family to do if anything should happen to him?

# Scene 6

**Narrator 2:** When Rigoberta returned to her village in the mountains, she learned about how her father had stood up to the government official. She was proud of him, but she was scared, too.

**Narrator 1:** The next day, Rigoberta's brother Petrocinio came rushing into the house.

**Petrocinio:** Father was arrested for protesting against the rich landowners! And the landowners gave money to the judge to give Father a long sentence in jail!

**Rigoberta:** What do we do now?

**Petrocinio:** We've got to go back to work on the plantations and try to make enough money to hire a lawyer.

**Narrator 2:** So Rigoberta and her brothers and sisters returned to work on the plantation. It took a year and two months, but they were finally able to get their father out of prison.

**Narrator 1:** Rigoberta's father was more determined than ever to help his people.

**Rigoberta:** I want to help you, Father. What can I do?

**Father:** Talk to people. Explain that together we can stand up for our rights and hold on to our land. It will be dangerous, but it is the only way.

**Narrator 2:** Rigoberta did as her father asked. The people of the village would gather to talk. They talked about the people who were killed. They talked about those who had their land taken away.

**Narrator 1:** At these meetings, Rigoberta would speak to the people.

**Rigoberta:** We must join together. We must demand decent wages for our work on the plantation. We deserve it!

**Narrator 2:** By the time Rigoberta was 16, she could speak many other Indian languages. She began organizing tribes around the country.

**Narrator 1:** She also learned to read and write in Spanish. She knew that she could not really help her people without those skills.

What was Rigoberta's message to her people?

# Scene

**Narrator 2:** One day, the army came to Rigoberta's village.

**Soldier:** Where is your father?

**Rigoberta:** He is away in another village.

**Soldier:** When he comes back—if he ever comes back—tell him he'd better watch out. Your whole family could disappear. Do you know what I mean?

**Rigoberta:** How can you say such things? How can you do this to us?

**Narrator 1:** Rigoberta had heard stories about people who had disagreed with the government and had mysteriously disappeared.

**Soldier:** Everyone knows that you and your

family are troublemakers.

**Rigoberta:** What do you mean?

**Soldier:** You put ideas into the heads of the other Indians. They used to do what they were told with no arguments. The people aren't happy anymore. From now on, the army is going to keep a very close eye on this village.

**Narrator 2:** But Rigoberta wasn't scared by the soldier's words. She was angry. She helped bring everyone in the village together. They made a plan to defend themselves, if the army attacked.

**Narrator 1:** They dug big holes outside their houses. If the soldiers tried to sneak up on them, they would fall in the traps. And they planned out escape routes. When the army arrived, they would find a ghost town.

How did the villagers plan to protect themselves?

# Scene 8

**Narrator 2:** But Rigoberta could not protect her own family. Her 16-year-old brother Petrocinio was kidnapped and handed over to the army. Rigoberta's family went to the army to try to free him.

**Army Captain:** The boy is a traitor to his country. He doesn't deserve to live. Go home. If you come back here again, you'll be arrested too.

**Narrator 1:** Weeks passed, and there was no word about Rigoberta's brother. One day, people in a neighboring village found his lifeless body in the town square.

**Army Captain:** You see. This is what happens to traitors who fight the government.

**Narrator 2:** Rigoberta could not stop her tears, but her mother did not cry.

**Rigoberta:** Mother, you are in such pain. Scream, do something. Don't keep it in.

**Mother:** If I start to cry it will be a bad example for the neighbors. Your brother tried to help us all. He gave his life for others. We need to keep up our struggle for our rights; we don't need tears.

**Rigoberta:** Well, I am going to work even harder for the rights my brother died for. I am going to honor the wishes of my father and keep working for justice, no matter what.

What might happen to Rigoberta if she keeps speaking out against the government?

# Scene 9

**Narrator 1:** Rigoberta continued to fight for Indian rights. And when her father was killed during a protest, she vowed to fight even harder.

**Narrator 2:** Soon after, Rigoberta's mother was kidnapped, tortured, and killed. As the tears started to run down her face, Rigoberta remembered her mother's words about remaining strong.

**Narrator 1:** So, Rigoberta kept fighting. She helped to organize a strike. Indian workers stopped working and demanded decent pay. Because she wouldn't stop fighting, she became a hunted woman in her own country. To escape death, she had to leave Guatemala and move to Mexico.

**Narrator 2:** When people heard about Rigoberta, they invited her to speak in countries around the world. Then one day, a writer came to visit her.

**Writer:** Rigoberta, tell me your story. I will help you share it with the world.

**Rigoberta:** Let's tell the story of an Indian girl who struggled to read and write. Make it a book about how proud she is to be a Quiché Indian. Let the world know how important it is to keep the old traditions and to fight for what is right.

**Narrator 1:** With help, Rigoberta Menchú wrote her book. In 1992, she was awarded the Nobel Peace Prize. She helped thousands of people. But she inspired millions.

Did Rigoberta's story inspire you? Why or why not?

# Epilogue

Rigoberta's book was published when she was 23 years old. Nine years later, she became the youngest person ever to receive the Nobel Peace Prize. She accepted the prize on behalf of all people struggling against poverty and racism. She dedicated it to the memory of her father.

After the book was published, some people said that not all of what Rigoberta had written was exactly true. Rigoberta admitted that she mixed other people's stories in with her own. She said that she was trying to show the suffering of her people—not just her own.

In 1993, after winning the Nobel Prize, Rigoberta was able to return to Guatamala. Today, she lives there with her family and still works for social justice.